ROYAL MAIL STEAMSHIP *TITANIC*

Published by Abdo & Daughters, 6537 Cecilia Circle, Bloomington, Minnesota 55435

Library bound edition distributed by Rockbottom Books, Pentagon Tower, P.O. Box 36036, Minneapolis, Minnesota 55435

Copyright © 1988 by Abdo Consulting Group, Inc., Pentagon Tower, P.O. Box 36036, Minneapolis, Minnesota 55435. International copyrights reserved in all countries. No part of this book may be reproduced in any form without written permission from the publisher. Printed in the United States.

Library of Congress Number: 88-71722   ISBN: 0-939179-42-3

Cover Photo by: Bettmann Archive Inc.
Inside Photos by:
    The Bettmann Archive, Inc.: pg. 7, 18, 20, 22, 24, 28
    Underwood Photo Archives: pg. 16

The Day of the Disaster

ROYAL MAIL STEAMSHIP *TITANIC*

Written By: Sue L. Hamilton
Edited By: John C. Hamilton

NOTE: The following is a fictional account based on factual data.

North Pocono Middle School
Moscow, Penna. 18444

H.M.S. TITANIC

MONDAY, APRIL 15th

12:05 a.m.
"I can't believe it — the 'unsinkable' ***Titanic*** is going down! The ship's builder guesses that we have no more than two hours to stay afloat. Captain Smith issues the orders: 'Uncover the lifeboats and call the passengers on deck. Prepare to abandon ship.'"

Just five days into her maiden voyage the H.M.S. ***Titanic,*** an oceanliner believed to be the safest ever made, struck an iceberg and sank into the icy depths of the Atlantic Ocean. Hundreds of lives were lost in one of the worst sea disasters ever recorded. When excitement turned to fear and tragedy, a ship's officer who survived told the frightening tale of ***Titanic's*** last hours.

FOREWORD - THE BEGINNING OF THE END

MARCH 31, 1909

Belfast, Ireland: Construction begins on the S.S. *Titanic* — a ship its owners say will be the greatest in size, luxury, speed, and safety.

MAY 31, 1911

More than 100,000 people watch the launching of the *Titanic,* the largest man-made object yet moved. Once in the water, work inside begins.

JANUARY 1912

Sixteen wooden lifeboats (plus four life rafts) are installed. The *Titanic* can carry up to 3,547 passengers and crew. Together, the lifeboats can hold only 1,178 passengers. Although the *Titanic* was to have 64 lifeboats, the owners and builders didn't believe they needed them - after all, they thought, *Titanic* was unsinkable.

FEBRUARY 1912
Work continues. Ship supplies begin to arrive: compasses, charts, navigation lamps, and 3,560 lifebelts.

APRIL 2, 1912
Titanic's first sea tests are run. She passes, and is given the OK to sail by the Board of Trade.

EVENING
Titanic sails to her dock in Southampton, England.

APRIL 3, 1912
On board, Senior Operator Jack Phillips and Junior Operator Harold Bride test the most powerful Marconi wireless radio ever used on any ship. Daytime range: 400 miles. Nighttime range: 1,200 miles.

APRIL 4-5, 1912
Inside the *Titanic,* work is still being completed. Tons of cargo and supplies are counted, listed, and stored.

APRIL 6, 1912

The crew is chosen. Many seamen are eager to sign on, but only the best will find jobs.

APRIL 8, 1912

Food is brought on board and stowed in huge refrigerators and storerooms. Among the supplies are 43 tons of fresh meat and fish, 40 tons of potatoes, 1,750 quarts of ice cream, 3 tons of butter, and 1,500 gallons of milk.

APRIL 9, 1912

All is made ready to sail the next morning.

TITANIC'S SAILING DAY

(From the diary of one of the ship's officers)

WEDNESDAY APRIL 10, 1912

6:00 a.m.
As I pull on my coat and prepare to go above, I can hear the singing and laughing of the crew as they come down to the ship. The day to set sail is finally here! Myself and several of the other officers have spent the night on board, keeping watch. When a ship costs $7.5 million dollars[1], and she holds millions of dollars in cargo, you've got to have lots of guards!

7:30 a.m.
After breakfast, I see Captian Edward John Smith coming aboard. He's been sailing for 43 years. I'll bet he never guessed that someday he'd command a ship four city blocks long and 11 stories high!

---

[1] Today, this equals almost $100 million dollars!

9:00 a.m.
We run through the required lifeboat drill. Two lifeboats are lowered, rowed around the dock, and raised back in place on deck. A half-hour drill. Seems like a waste of time.

10:00 a.m.
Passengers begin arriving. From millionaires to tennis pros to common steerage passengers, the lot of them will have the best trip possible aboard this ship.

I've heard we won't have a full load of passengers. Good. Less work for the crew. We've enough to do just try to figure out the layout of the ship. Below-decks is the worst — it seems like miles of twisting mazes. Since the cabins aren't numbered in order, the stewards will have their hands full just finding all the 3rd class cabins.

10:30 a.m.
FIRE! Chief Engineer Bell and the captain discuss a coal fire that's burning in one of the boiler rooms. The engineer says everything is under control. The captain believes him. Of course, what's the captain to do, stop *Titanic's* sailing? Only a disaster would cause that.

12:00 Noon
Titanic's huge whistles sing out, screaming to the world that the largest oceanliner on the North Atlantic is ready to set sail!

12:15 p.m.
Just as we get under way, a loose ship is spotted drifting towards us! It's going to be close...

1:30 p.m.
We've missed a collision with the American liner, *New York.* Even at our dead-slow speed, the waves from *Titanic* caused the other ship to break her ropes. A collision would have meant several days delay, but thanks to Captain Smith, Pilot Bowyer, and a quick-thinking tugboat commander, both ships are OK, and we're finally underway.

6:00 p.m.
We've reached our first stop — Cherbourg, France. Twenty-two passengers get off and 270 new passengers come aboard. The stay is short. By 8:10 p.m. we're underway again.

THURSDAY, APRIL 11, 1912
12:00 Noon

Queenstown, Ireland; our last stop before New York. An additional 120 passengers come aboard. Seven get off.

The ship's list shows 2,227 passengers and crew. We're licensed to carry at least 1,000 more. This will be an easy run compared to future trips when we have a full passenger load.

Traveled Noon Thursday - Noon Friday: 386 Miles.

FRIDAY, APRIL 12, 1912

The passengers are enjoying everything there is to do: a swimming pool, gym, squash & racquetball courts, library, Turkish baths, smoking rooms, and open & glassed-in decks. Plus, the huge kitchen, bakery, barber shop, private restaurants, and small hospital give the passengers every luxury and safety feature available.

11:00 p.m.

Our wireless radio has broken down! We're cut off from the world. Phillips and Bride will be working all night to get it fixed.

Traveled Noon Friday - Noon Saturday: 519 Miles.

SATURDAY, APRIL 13, 1912
5:00 a.m.
I understand that the wireless is repaired. There are hundreds of messages coming in and ready to be sent out. As tired as they are, the operators will have to stay on duty.

10:00 a.m.
As he has done every day, Captain Smith checks the ship. Myself and the other officers follow behind him, each of us giving our reports. Engineer Bell states that the coal fire is out. At least we won't have to call on the New York Fire Department when we reach port. We walk through the hull's 16 watertight rooms, each divided by steel walls. This is what makes **Titanic** unsinkable. One certainly feels safe aboard this ship. It's as I overhead one crewman state: "Even God, himself, could not sink this ship."

1:00 p.m.
The passengers like knowing our daily mileage. Several have asked me if we're trying to set a record. I hate to disappoint them, but **Titanic** is built for luxury, not speed. Of course, the captain has us going fast enough to make sure we get to New York on time.

4:00 p.m.
It has become quite cold in the last few hours. Most of the passengers have gone to their cabins. As we sail north we'll have to keep a sharp lookout for storms and ice.

Traveled Noon Saturday - Noon Sunday: 546 Miles.

SUNDAY, APRIL 14, 1912
Dawn
Bright and clear. The sea is like glass...almost *too* smooth.

9:00 a.m.
Captain Smith posts a message from the steamship *Caronia:* "Captain, **Titanic** — Westbound steamers report bergs, growlers and field ice (in your area)..." The lookouts will have their work cut out for them tonight, although the evening is still very clear. We should have no problems.

5:00-7:00 p.m.
The temperature has dropped even more: from 43° to 33° F.

7:30 p.m.
The wireless operators report overhearing the liner **Californian** warning the freighter **Antillian** of ice. Looks like we're in for some zig-zagging through the bergs.

9:00 p.m.
The captain is on deck telling the lookouts to keep a sharp watch for ice. He hasn't ordered the engines slowed, though. As most captains do, he'll reduce speed only when an iceberg is spotted, and then change course as needed.

9:40 p.m.
I stopped by the wireless room. Phillips has hundreds of messages to send, plus there's countless more coming in.
(NOTE: During this time, the liner **Mesaba** sends word of icebergs all around **Titanic's** location. This message never reaches the bridge.)

10:00 p.m.
Lookouts Frederick Fleet and Reginald Lee are climbing to the crow's nest. It's still clear, but they'll have to keep a sharp eye out for ice.

10:30 p.m.
(NOTE: *Rappahannock* warns *Titanic* of ice.)

10:55 p.m.
Operator Phillips is sending messages to Cape Race, Newfoundland, Canada. The *Californian* cuts in: "We're stopped and surrounded by ice." Phillips, tired and mad, wires back: "Shut up. I'm busy with Cape Race."

(NOTE: That's the last message heard from *Californian's* operator. He shuts down his radio.)

11:30 p.m.
The ship has sailed into a strange haze. Lookouts Fleet and Lee are straining to see what's ahead of us. They do not have binoculars. It's believed that the glasses limit how far lookouts can see side-to-side. I think at least one of them could use a pair tonight.

11:40 p.m.
It's late. A quiet time on the bridge...Wait! Three loud rings! It's Fleet calling from the crow's nest: "Iceberg right ahead!"

Everyone scrambles. First Officer William Murdoch issues our orders: "Full speed astern! Hard-a-starboard! Close the water-tight doors! Alert the captain!"

11:41 p.m.
There's no time to stop. We wait for the impact... All we feel is a slight lurch. Some pieces of ice rain down on the forward deck.

11:55 p.m.
It looks like we're OK, although the captain is going below to inspect. It'll probably mean a new paint job on one side, but that should be all.

12:00 Midnight
DISASTER! The iceberg has cut a 300-foot slice into the right side of **Titanic.** Sea water is pouring in. With this much of the ship flooding, she'll never be able to stay afloat, even with the water-tight doors shut!

MONDAY, APRIL 15TH
12:05 a.m.

I can't believe it — the 'unsinkable' **Titanic** is going down! The ship's builder guesses that we have no more than two hours to stay afloat. Captain Smith issues the orders: "Uncover the lifeboats and call the passengers on deck. Prepare to abandon ship."

12:15 a.m.

The captain has told the wireless operators to send out a call for help. Phillips taps out: "Come at once. We have struck a berg. MGY CQD Position 41° 46′ N, 50° 14′ W."

(NOTE: "MGY" is **Titanic's** call letters. "CQD" is a standard call for help.)

12:25 a.m.

The order is passed: "Load the lifeboats." Crewmen are rushing from cabin to cabin, handing out lifebelts and getting the passengers up on deck. No one knows where to go; we've never even had a boat drill. Plus, there's room for only 1,178 aboard the lifeboats — over 1,000 seats short. Help has to come quickly.

Women and children first.

12:30 a.m.

The operators are unable to reach the *Californian* — she's only 10-20 miles away.

(NOTE: The *Californian's* operator had shut down his radio at 11:00 p.m.)

12:33 a.m.

Carpathia sends word that she is on the way. It'll take her four hours to reach us. We don't have that much time.

12:40 a.m.

Operator Phillips continues to send out calls for help. We're the first ship to use the new distress call: "SOS."

Ships throughout the area have signaled that they are on their way, but they're all from 50-500 miles away — too far off to help. If only we could reach the *Californian!*

12:45 a.m.

The first lifeboat is lowered — only 28 people are aboard, although there's room for 37 more. Still, we've got to keep things moving.

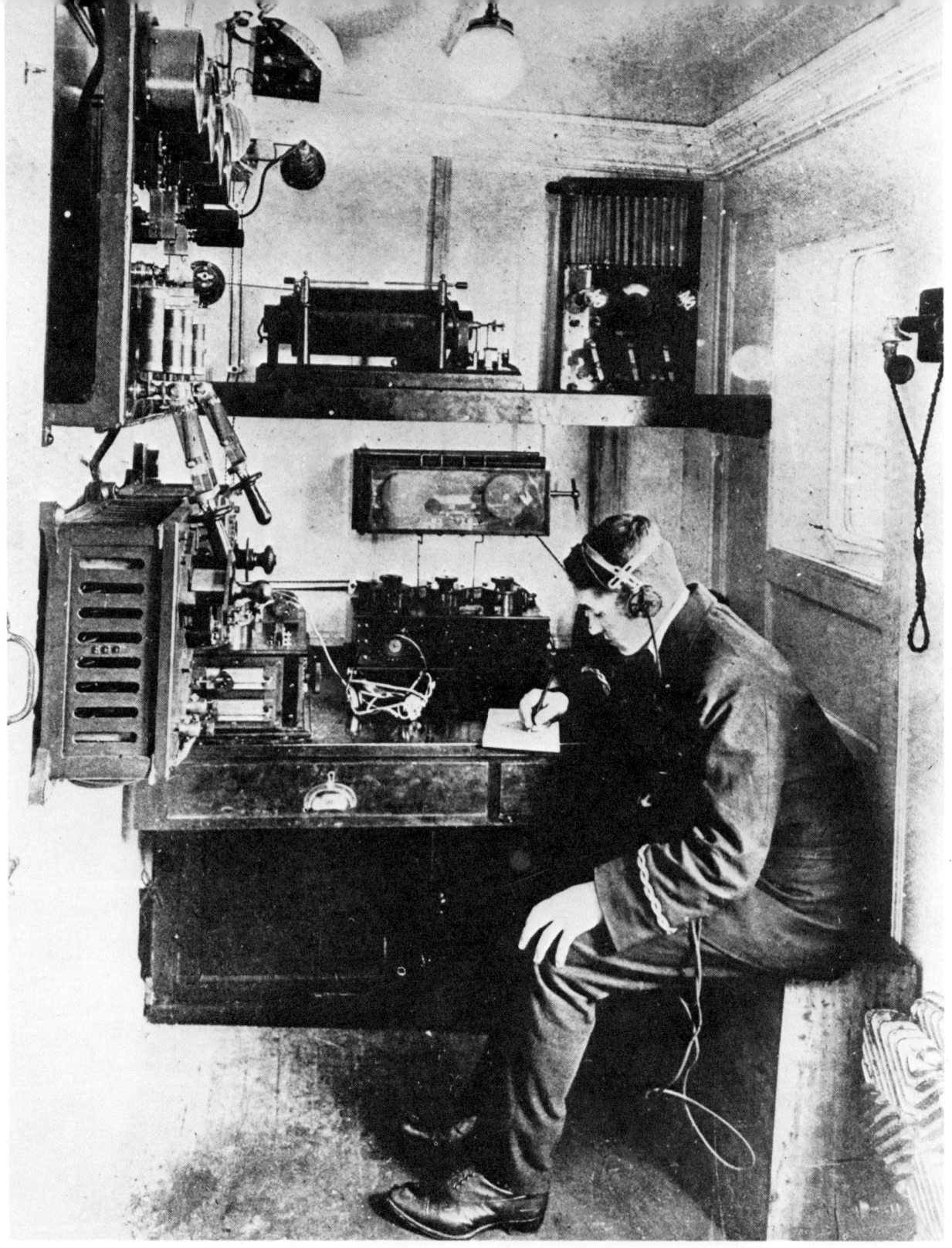

Re-enactment of the scene in the wireless room of the S.S. Carpathia where distress signals were first heard.

On deck, Bandmaster Wallace Hartley and his seven musicians play some ragtime tunes to keep people calm. Quartermaster Rowe is ordered to fire distress-signal rockets into the air, one every five minutes. It's like a strange party as crew and passengers gather near the lifeboats. The band plays and rockets light up the sky as though it were day.

1:15 a.m.
The last rocket is launched. We can see a ship on the horizon, but we're unable to reach it by wireless. Two of the other officers are on deck trying Morse lamp signals. It could be the ***Californian*** . . . She's turning away! Why doesn't she see us? This ship may have been our last chance for a complete rescue.

1:40 a.m.
Titanic is sinking fast. It's now clear to everyone that she's going down. Lifeboat loading is becoming dangerous as people panic and press forward. Myself and the other officers have made it clear: women and children first. If there are no more women and children nearby, men may get on board.

The sinking of the luxury ocean liner, Titanic, after its collision with an iceberg, April 14, 1912.

2:00 a.m.
The last wooden lifeboat reaches the water; only the canvas life rafts are left. With **Titanic's** bow almost completely flooded, it's going to be almost impossible to get those rafts launched. The band is still playing, but now it's a hymn: "Nearer My God to Thee."

2:05 a.m.
As we both climb into one of the canvas life rafts, wireless operator Bride tells me Captain Smith's last words to him: "You've done your duty, now it's every man for himself." Phillips has stayed at the radio to send one last message: "Come quick, our engine room is flooded up to the boilers."

2:10 a.m.
From our raft, we watch as the ship's bow goes under. Everything not nailed down slides forward in an ear-splitting crash. The last life raft is washed overboard and lands upside-down in the water.

2:15 a.m.
She's going down! Terrified screams echo across the water as those unable to escape the ship are washed overboard into the freezing sea.

2:19 a.m.
Titanic's bow is completely under water. Her lights are still shining, giving off a greenish-glow. Suddenly they flash off . . . back on . . . and then off for the last time.

2:20 a.m.
For several seconds, she stops. Then slowly the "unsinkable" *Titanic*, just 5 days into her first voyage, sinks into a watery grave in the icy cold depths of the Atlantic Ocean.

EPILOGUE — THE END OF THE END

2:25 a.m.
People are afraid that the swimmers will overturn their boats. Most rowers will not go back to rescue those in the water.

3:00 a.m.
The cries have stopped. The lifebelts have kept the swimmers afloat, but the freezing water has killed them.

3:30 a.m.
RESCUE! The liner *Carpathia* is headed towards the first of our lifeboats. She's moving slowly — the entire area is filled with icebergs.

5:40 a.m.
(NOTE: Captain Lord, aboard the *Californian*, finally learns of the *Titanic's* disaster. He immediately sets course for the ship's last known position.)

8:30 a.m.
The last boatload of survivors is brought on board *Carpathia*. Captain Smith is not among us. He has gone down with the ship.

The *Californian* has just arrived . . . too late. Tragically too late. Our next job: counting survivors.

9:00 a.m.
Other ships are now arriving. *Carpathia's* Captain Rostrom has asked the *Californian* and others to look for possible survivors. We're heading for New York.

Afternoon

We've finished our count. ***Titanic's*** deadly truth:

$$\begin{array}{r} 2{,}227 \text{ passengers \& crew} \\ -\underline{705} \text{ saved} \\ 1{,}522 \text{ KILLED} \end{array}$$

Relatives waiting for the survivors of the Titanic.

TUESDAY & WEDNESDAY, APRIL 16 & 17, 1912

Carpathia's wireless operator has been on duty for over 24 hours, sending news to the mainland. We are carrying *Titanic's* operator, Bride, to the radio room to help. His feet are crushed and frostbitten, but he's needed to help send out names of the survivors.

THURSDAY, APRIL 18, 1912
Dusk

During a heavy rainstorm, we sail into New York Harbor. The *Carpathia* goes by her own pier and on to *Titanic's*, where the lifeboats are lowered — all that is left of the newest, largest, most beautiful, and "safest" oceanliner ever built.

9:30 p.m.

The first of our group walks onto the pier. Thousands of people have come down to the harbor. A greeting that should have been a celebration is now a story of sadness and tragedy.

WEEKS AND MONTHS FOLLOWING THE DISASTER

I am sailing aboard another vessel. I still dream about that awful night. Still, **Titanic's** sinking has brought about many good changes:

- There's a lifeboat space for every person on board every ship.
- Every ship must have a lifeboat drill every time she sails.
- Captains listen carefully to all ice warnings. Ships must steer clear of the area or slow down.
- During the winter in the North Atlantic, all ships now follow a more southerly route.
- A ship's wireless radio must be switched on 24 hours a day.
- An International Ice Patrol has been formed. (NOTE: Today, the Coast Guard performs this duty.)

We can at least take comfort in knowing that, with these changes, the 1,522 people who died on the **Titanic** did not perish for nothing. And no one will forget the disastrous day of April 15, 1912 — **Titanic's** final moments in time.

POSTSCRIPT

MONDAY, SEPTEMBER 1, 1985
1:40 a.m.
After 73 years, American Dr. Robert Ballard of the Woods Hole Oceanographic Institution, and French scientist Jean-Louis Michel, have discovered ***Titanic's*** final resting place: Sitting upright more than two miles beneath the ocean's surface, broken in half and laying about 10 miles from her last stated position.

1986
In the months following the discovery, U.S. and French scientists will dive down to photograph and explore the ***Titanic***. Surprisingly, they do not find a "300 foot gash" in her side. It is now believed that the hull's steel plates broke apart, causing the ship to flood.

Whatever the cause, ***Titanic's*** tragic ending will never be forgotten.

SOURCES CONSULTED

Ballard, Robert D. "How We Found *Titanic*," **National Geographic,** December 1985, pp. 696-719.

Ballard, Robert D. "A Long Last Look at *Titanic*" **National Geographic,** December 1986, pp. 698-727.

Bower, Bruce. "Return to the *Titanic*: Gash is dashed" **Science News,** August 9, 1986, p. 86.

Buckley, William F., Jr. "On The Right" **National Review,** October 9, 1987, pp. 70-71.

Eaton, John P., and Haas, Charles A. ***Titanic* Triumph and Tragendy.** New York & London: W.W. Norton & Company Inc., 1986.

Lord, Walter. **A Night To Remember.** New York: Holt, Rinehart and Winston, 1966.

Lord, Walter. **The Night Lives On.** New York: William Morrow and Company, Inc., 1986.

Oxford, Edward. "The *Titanic* Remembered" **American History Illustrated,** April 1986, pp. 8-32.

Oxford, Edward. "*Titanic*: First Pyramid in the Sea" **American History Illustrated,** April 1986, pp. 33-37.

Wallechinsky, David, and Wallace, Irving. **The People's Almanac.** New York: Doubleday & Company, Inc., 1975.

Winocour, Jack. **The Story of the *Titanic* As Told By Its Survivors.** New York: Dover Publications, Inc., 1960.